Deer-Resistant Gardening in the Midwest

Fall Planting Edition

Sue Monson

Almennigen Enterprises

Contents

Dedication

To my boyfriend, Ross, for his kind support, and, indirectly, to the deer that keep visiting his backyard, inspiring me to do something about it.

Chapter One

Introduction

WELL, YOU'VE DONE YOUR planting this spring, with the help of my first book, and you're ready to plant the flower bulbs, shrubs, and trees this fall to prepare your yard for a wonderful year. The deer have avoided your garden because you chose to plant things they don't like, whether it be smelly, fuzzy, or grayish. Now you know the deer can be outsmarted, at least for the most part. Keep in mind, in the early spring when they are especially hungry, snow is still covering the ground, and few plants have surfaced yet, they will eat anything they can find. Another important incentive to keeping deer out of your yard is the deer ticks that can carry Lyme Disease.

There are several ways to keep deer out if you don't want to share your garden goodies. Let's review the options.

Chapter Two

Physical Protection

IF YOU WANT TO have some plants that deer (and you) consider delicious, you must protect them. A large dog will work as long as he is outside, but deer will see when he is inside. Then the deer will attack their favorite plants. Deer are kinda smart. If you want to have your dog inside at night for personal protection and when the weather gets chilly, you need to consider physical barriers. A fence can also keep a dog with wanderlust or an irresistible curiosity within your yard. Deer can easily jump anything up to seven feet high if they can see a nice landing area. If you bury a fence half a foot into the ground, you can prevent burrowing creatures from entering as well.

Deer will not jump a fence if they can't see a safe landing spot, so two fences six feet tall and four feet apart will keep the deer away, but they make your yard look like a battleground. I suppose it is a battleground but who wants that look?

If you have tasty seedlings that you may have started inside, you can put a shorter fence around them and make a section of extra fencing into a roof. This roof means you can't weed them unless you have an easy way to remove the roof, so lay a ground cover before planting.

Another option is to electrify the fence. Deer will keep testing it, so don't turn it off for any length of time. Be sure to check local ordinances before installing any fence, especially an electric fence.

Putting fishing lines around the garden will help deter deer, as they can't see it after dark. The lines might be a good option paired with a dog who is outside during the day.

If you need to protect your young trees from damage caused by deer rubbing their antlers against the bark, you can erect a fence around the tree.

You can tell what animal is damaging your tree by looking at the marks. Of course, rabbit and rodent marks are lower than deer marks. Torn jagged looking tears in the bark are from deer. Deer have no upper incisors, so they must grab and tear. Squirrels and rabbits leave a clean-cut mark about 45 degrees from vertical. Rabbit marks are usually the width of a spoon, whereas rodent marks look like they were made with a fork. All can cause permanent damage to expensive trees.

It goes without saying (oops, I said it) that you must keep these fences in good repair. Deer constantly check their boundaries, just like children. Make sure your metal fencing is galvanized and your propylene fencing is UV-protected to ensure a long-lasting barrier. Black coated wire mesh fencing is almost invisible in the yard. Make sure your fencing is rated for more than eight hundred pounds breaking load. Deer are strong. Wooden privacy fences are an option if they are tall enough to prevent deer from seeing the other side. The gate will need to be deer proof as well. A greenhouse is always an option.

Chapter Three

Chemical Repellent

You can utilize chemical deer repellants if you don't want to look at a fence but still want your tasty veggies. You can purchase deer repellant spray, which must be applied repeatedly, as the rain will wash it off. One which is supposed to be good is called Liquid Fence Deer and Rabbit Repellent. If you want to make one yourself, you'll need something that smells like a predator- a wolf maybe. Hunting stores can usually supply what you need.

Chapter Four

Deer-Resistant Plants

THE EASIEST OPTION IS to plant stuff that deer don't especially like. Anything with a strong flavor, like onions or garlic, or a strong odor, like marigolds, will encourage deer to try next door instead. Furry or spiky leaves irritate their sensitive noses, as will thorns. Deer don't like gray-colored leaves. Using deer-resistant plants around the garden perimeter will discourage deer from tasting more desirable plants farther in. Deer are creatures of habit, and they will remember the best plants from last year and hit them again. They will also remember the location of plants they dislike.

Set realistic goals when it comes to deer damage. A 50% reduction in damage is great, but 30% is average. Deer can jump up to twelve feet in the air and squeeze through gaps as small as seven and a half inches if they are highly motivated, i.e. running for their lives.

Here in the Midwest, we get large ranges of temperatures from season to season. We are in Zones 3-8. The Zone is determined by how cold it gets in the winter. Be aware of how hot it gets in the summer too. When I lived in Minnesota, I was amazed that a place that got sooooo cold in the winter could get so hot and humid in the summer. When I lived in Upstate New York (yes, I moved around a lot) it didn't get as cold in the winter or as hot in the summer.

When going through the list, note that some sub-species are deer resistant, while other subspecies are not. When in doubt, ask your local garden center specialist for advice. When available, I put the Rutgers rating down. "A" means the plant is rarely damaged by deer, "B" means it is seldom severely damaged. I didn't bother to put anything in category C or D into the table since those are not deer-resistant.

Chapter Five

Images and Descriptions of Deer-Resistant Plants

Abelia, Glossy (abelia x grandiflora) (a-BEE-lee-uh ex gran-dih-FLOR-uh)

Glossy Abelia is a rounded, spreading, multi-stemmed shrub in the Honeysuckle family. It grows on gracefully arching branches from two to four feet tall. If the stems die to the ground in a harsh winter, the plant survives. Flowering will still occur, but only bloom on smaller plants that reach a height of a foot to a foot and a half. Clusters of fragrant, white-tinged, bell-shaped flowers appear over a long bloom period - late spring to fall. Glossy, dark green leaves turn purplish-bronze in autumn. Easily grown in average, medium, well-drained soil in full sun to partial shade in Zones 6-9. Best flowering is in full sun. Prefers moist, organically rich soils that drain well. Somewhat evergreen in the South, but generally deciduous in the Midwest, stems may suffer substantial damage (including dying to the ground) in cold winters. Significant stem damage can be expected when winter temperatures approach zero degrees F. Best suited to a protected location. Blooms on new wood, so prune as needed (e.g., remove stems lost to winter and, if desired, cut to the ground) in late winter to early spring. Rutgers rating B.

Aconite, Winter (eranthis hyemalis) (eer-RAN-this hy-EH-may-liss)

Winter Aconite is best grown in organically rich, medium moisture, well-drained soils in full sun to partial shade. It's best planted under deciduous trees to enjoy the full sun at the time of bloom, but acquire increasing shade as overhead trees leaf out. This plant needs consistent moisture year-round (albeit less in summer and fall) even though the plant goes dormant by late spring. It may self-seed and naturalize over time in optimum growing conditions. However, it's best left undisturbed once planted. One of the first signs of spring, this rugged plant often sends it's shoots up through the snow. Green leaves emerge after the flowers. Max height is one foot, Zones 3-7, full sun, yellow flowers in the early spring. Rutgers rating A. Some sources suggest Aconite to help pain, fright, fever, or restlessness.

Allium (allium) (AL-ee-um)

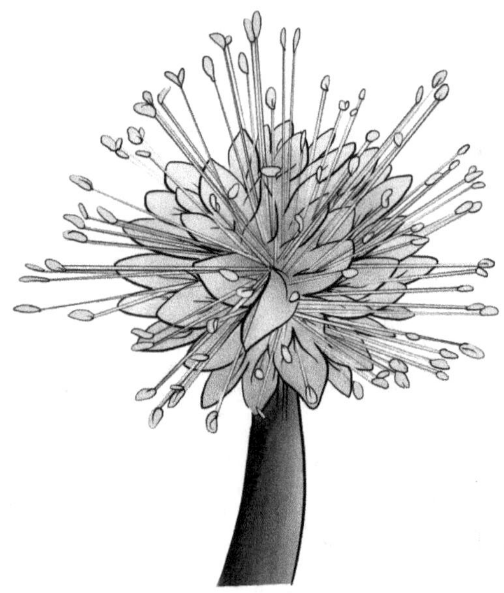

Anything in the Allium family is an onion with the odor and taste that go along with all onions. Deer do not like strong odors and tastes so will generally leave this alone. Bulb rot may occur in overly moist soils. Slugs can attack young plants. Mildew, rust, and leaf spots may appear. Watch for onion maggots and thrips (tiny insects with fringed wings). Bulbs are winter hardy only to Zone 5 or 6, so Midwesteners need to bring them in over the winter. Max height eight feet, Zones 4-9, full sun or partial sun, yellow-green blooms in spring through fall. Some herbal references cite Allium to relieve cold symptoms.

Allspice, Carolina (calycanthus floridus) (kal-ee-KAN-thus FLOR-id-us)

Carolina Allspice shrubs are dense, rounded, and deciduous, with a habit of spreading by sending out suckers. They grow six to nine feet (less frequently to twelve feet) tall with an equal or slightly greater spread. They feature very fragrant brown to reddish-brown flowers (two inches across) that bloom at the ends of short branchlets in May. Be sure to buy these when they are blooming, as the quality and quantity of scent vary from plant to plant. Some people describe the scent as a mix of Pineapple, Strawberry, and Banana. Even the leaves are fragrant when bruised. If the fragrance isn't enough to repel the deer, who don't like strong scents, the leaves are hairy as well. Traditional medicine suggests Allspice can help indigestion.

Barberry (berberis) (BUR-bur-is)

Japanese Barberry, also called Oregon Grape-Holly (mahonia japonica), is considered invasive in the Midwest, but other varieties of Barberry (berberis) are ok to use. Max height eight feet, Zones 3-9, full sun or partial sun, yellow flowers that bloom in the spring, Rutgers rating A. Some Barberry varieties might not be deer-tolerant, so make sure before buying, as there are 400 varieties. Buy two plants so they can pollinate and produce berries. All Barberry varieties feature spiny stems which bother deer. Some sources suggest Barberry bark is useful for urinary tract infection pain as it contains the alkaloid berberine.

Bayberry, Northern (myrica pensylvanica) (MIR-i-ka pen-sill-VAN-ee-ka)

Northern Bayberry is a dense shrub that tolerates salty conditions well, like seashores and along roads. If you want berries, plant a male shrub beside as many female shrubs as you want. The berries are coated with a waxy substance that is used to make candles. The wax and the grayish-green leaves both contribute to its deer resistance, as well as the fact that the leaves are aromatic when crushed. Max height twenty feet, Zones 3-7, full sun or partial sun, Rutgers rating A, yellowish-green flowers in the spring only on male plants.

Beautyberry (callicarpa) (kal-ee-KAR-puh)

Beautyberry plants prefer soil like native forest floors- moist clay or sand with lots of organic matter. It fruits best in full sun but will survive partial sun with less fruit. Even if the winter kills the part of the plant which is above ground, it will come back in the spring and still bear fruit. Zones 5-8, Rutgers rating B, purple or pink flowers in spring and summer.

Beech, American (fagus grandifoia) (FAG-us grand-dih-FOH-lee-uh)

The American Beech tree is native to eastern North America and is known for its smooth grayish bark. The tree is oval shaped and can reach fifty feet high and forty feet wide. It likes moist, well-drained soil best, and will not do well in wet or poorly-drained soil. It is difficult to transplant and doesn't do well in urban settings. The ovate to elliptical leaves turn golden bronze in the fall. In late spring, greenish flowers appear in drooping clusters on males and short spikes on females. The female blooms ripen into triangular edible nuts. It prefers Zones 3-9 and full sun to part shade.

Birch (betula) (BET-yoo-luh)

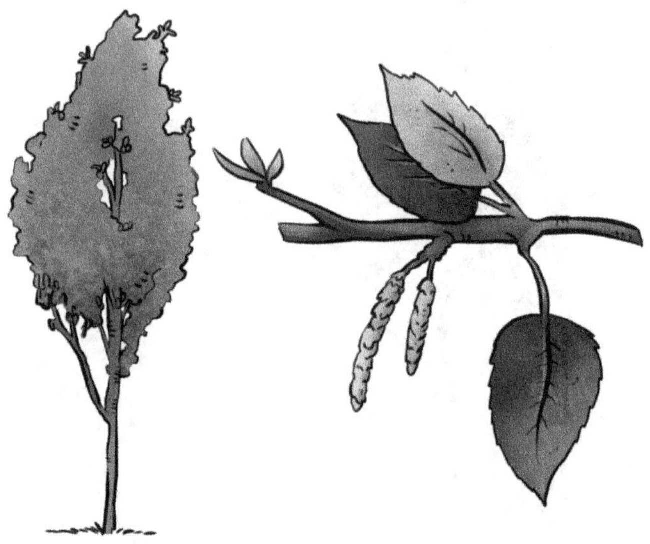

The grayish-white bark of Birch trees reminds me of northern Michigan, where my mom grew up. They prefer snow in winter, moist, acidic, sandy, or rocky soils. Use a soaker hose if you are far enough south to reach above 75 deg F in the summer, which covers most of the Midwest. You can also use mulch to keep the moisture from evaporating. It can reach twenty feet in height and usually does not require pruning. Yellow-green flowers appear in the spring. Zones 3-7, full sun or partial sun.

Boxwood, Common (buxus sempervirens) (BUK-sus sem-per-VY-renz)

Boxwood is a great choice for a hedge between properties, but make sure it has some shade and is protected from the wind. Otherwise, it will turn bronze, which isn't very pretty. The flowers are insignificant, so don't count on them brightening up the green leaves. Prune them after the last frost to allow air circulation, thus avoiding pests. They can reach thirty feet high if left alone, but pruning is recommended to prevent them from looking scraggly. Zones 4-8 or 5-8, depending on the source. Rutgers rating A, and rabbit-resistant as well. They prefer partial sun but will tolerate shade if you don't mind an airier bush.

Bugbane (actaea simplex) (ak-TEE-uh SIM-plecks)

Bugbane is another plant with an odd name. This time it is well deserved. The strong odor does repel insects. It is also called Cohosh from an Algonquin word meaning rough, referring to the blooms. This odor is why it repels deer as well. It prefers full shade or at least partial shade and likes moist soil. It dries out easily and can scorch in the sun. It performs best when sheltered from the wind. It is slow to establish so be patient with this one. The white spiky flowers show up in late summer, and the plant can reach four feet high, eventually. Zones 4-9.

Bush, Butterfly (buddleia) (BUD-lee-uh)

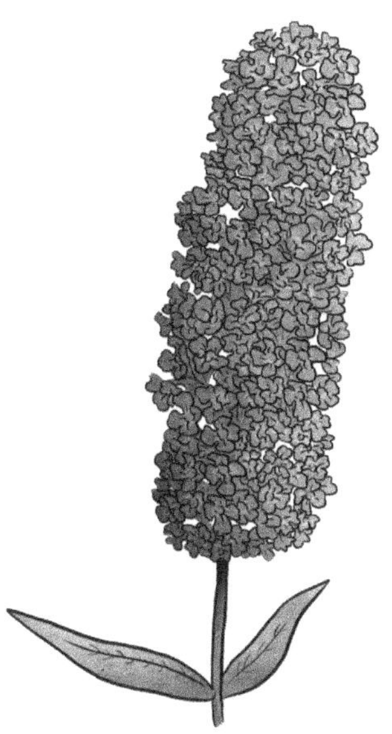

The Butterfly Bush is heaven to butterflies and bees, but be careful or it will take over the place. It spreads by self-seeding, so gather the seed pods before they split open and disperse their seeds. It has been declared invasive in some states, but not in the Midwest. Prune it down to the ground in late fall. It loves full sun but will tolerate partial sun if you don't expect too much of it. It doesn't like wet feet so make sure the soil is well-draining. Purple or pink flowers bloom in the summer, depending on the particular cultivar. It is rabbit-resistant and can reach fifteen feet tall and fifteen feet wide, with showy flowers arching over the leaves. Zones 5-10, Rutgers rating A.

Bush, Lily of the Valley (pieris japonica) (pee-AIR-iss juh-PON-ih-kuh)

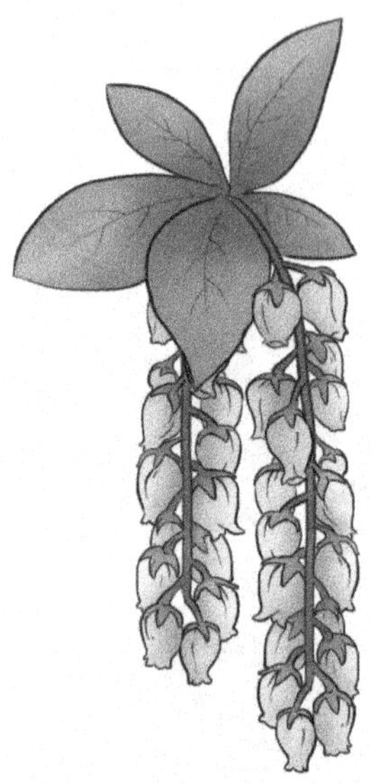

The Lily of the Valley Bush (pieris japonica) is not the same as the Lily of the Valley (convallaria majus). This bush originated in Japan and eastern China and can also be called Japanese Pieris. It grows best when sheltered from the afternoon sun and the wind. Flower buds are set in late summer for the following year, so prune this one directly after blooming or not at all. Keep an eye out for lace bug infestations. It can reach twelve feet tall and eight feet wide in ideal conditions. The white flowers droop in clusters in the spring. Remove spent flowers immediately to make room for those buds for next year. Zones 5-8. Leaves and flowers are poisonous upon ingestion.

Bush, Spice (lindera benzoin) (lin-DEER-ruh ben-ZOH-in)

The Spice Bush is native to the Midwest and shows off in the fall when the leaves turn gold. It can grow up to twelve feet tall and twelve feet wide if left alone. If you want berries, make sure to have both male and female plants. Leaves are aromatic when crushed, which is why deer don't like this particular plant. The larva (caterpillar stage) of the Spice Bush Swallowtail Butterfly feeds on the leaves of this bush. This plant can tolerate full shade, but it will be more open in structure. Fall color is better when in full sun. The spring flowers are greenish-yellow. Zones 4-9.

Camas, Large (camassia leichtlinii) (kuh-MAS-ee-uh leekt-LIN-ee-eye)

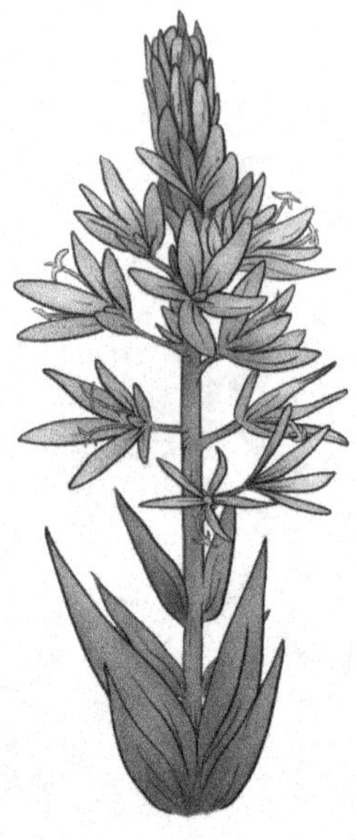

The Large Camas plant produces white, cream, blue, and purple blooms, depending on the plant. They last from spring through summer but don't show up until the third or fourth year if grown from seed. It will tolerate dry conditions after the flowers are gone. It is native to the western US. The name comes from the word kamas or quamash from Native American use of the bulb for food. It can grow to four feet tall and two feet wide. Zones 4-8, Rutgers rating B.

Candytuft (iberis sempervirens) (eye-BEER-is sem-per-VY-renz)

Candytuft is a low evergreen shrub that requires full sun and good drainage. It is drought-tolerant but will develop problems if the roots stay wet. Mulch the plant in winter to avoid sun scorching and desiccation. Cut back about a third after flowering to keep it compact and encourage new growth. The white flowers may cover all the leaves, fading gradually to light pink. Plants reach about a foot high and a foot and a half wide. They spread by stems rooting where they touch the ground. Rabbit-resistant. Zones 3-8, Rutgers rating B.

Cedar, Red Eastern (juniperus virginiana) (jew-NIP-er-us vir-jin-ee-AN-uh)

The Eastern Red Cedar tolerates a wide range of soil conditions but doesn't like having wet feet constantly. It has the best drought resistance of any conifer native to the eastern US. It has gray to reddish-brown bark that can peel off in mature trees. Heartwood is reddish-brown and commonly used for cedar chests. Dark bluish-green scale-like foliage can turn brownish-green in the winter. The female trees produce small round berry-like cones which attract birds. Plant male and female trees together for best results. Avoid planting near Apple trees as Cedar Apple rust is common. This dense tree can grow to seventy-five feet tall and is tolerant of heat, drought, salt, and cold. Zones 2-9. Rutgers rating B.

Cherry, Flowering, Japanese (prunus serrulata) (PROO-nus ser-yoo-LAY-tuh)

The Japanese Flowering Cherry Tree is a familiar sight in the spring in Japan and Washington, DC, but will grow anywhere in Zones 5-8 if it has full sun. The white to pink flowers are beautiful and cover the entire tree in the spring. The cherries come later and are tasty. The tree can reach twenty-five feet tall and just as wide, can tolerate a little shade but loves the sun. It is susceptible to many insect and disease pests, so be aware. Rutgers rating B.

Chestnut, American (castanea dentata) (kas-TAN-nee-uh den-TAY-tuh)

The American Chestnut tree grows best in Zones 5-8 to a height of fifty feet and a spread just as impressive. The yellow-white blooms arrive in June, larger in male blooms but not very impressive anywhere. It prefers full sun and medium moisture soil. This is a high-maintenance tree as it's prone to blight. There is ongoing research into blight-resistant varieties, but the blight has decimated the entire American population. Small nuts are sweet and edible but are encased in spiny burrs.

Chokecherry, Red (aronia arbutifolia) (ar-ROH-nee-uh ar-bew-tih-FOH-lee-uh)

The Red Chokecherry gets its name from its berries being so astringent that anyone who tries to eat one will choke. The berries do make a tasty jam, however. It can tolerate wet, boggy soil, making it ideal for along river beds. It does spread rapidly, so watch it. It will grow to ten feet tall and six feet wide. The white to light pink flowers appear in spring, followed by red fruits. The leaves turn bright red in the fall, rivaling the Burning Bush for fall color. It can tolerate partial sun but does best in full sun. Zones 4-9. Rutgers rating B.

Coralberry "Snowberry" (symphoricarpos albus) (sim-for-ee-KAR-poss AL-bus)

The Coralberry shrub, also known as Waxberry, is easily grown in average soil in full sun or part sun, with full sun yielding the best fruit production. It adapts to many soil conditions including poor ones. Prune as needed in late winter or early spring. Native to Eastern North America, it grows to a rounded shrub about six feet in any direction in Zones 3-7. Summer pink blooms precede pale green berries that lighten to white by early autumn. Birds don't especially like the berries, so they add interest to the winter landscape. Their tendency to spread by suckering makes them ideal for erosion control on rocky slopes, but be careful to keep them contained. Don't eat the berries! They're poisonous.

Cotoneaster (cotoneaster) (kot-on-ee-ASS-ter)

Cotoneaster shrubs originated in Siberia and China, so you know they can handle Minnesota winters. Rated for Zones 4-7, they grow to ten feet high and just as wide. Seeds or cuttings spread them. Once established, they can withstand some drought conditions and can tolerate poor soil. Mulch the ground under the plant to discourage weeds from coming up within the plant, where they are hard to reach. Flowers are small and white with a pink tinge and are followed by small oval fruits. The redeeming quality of this plant is its impressive orange-red color in the fall. It is rabbit-resistant as well. It likes full sun but can do just as well in partial sun conditions. Rutgers rating B.

Cotoneaster   Bearberry   (cotoneaster   dammeri)   (kot-on-ee-ASS-ter DAM-mer-ee)

Cotoneaster Bearberry plants are a subspecies of Cotoneaster that are ground covers, only a foot high at the most. They spread easily and must be pruned. But if you often forget to water your plants, this is the one for you. Once established, it rarely needs watering. White flowers with purple anthers in spring/summer are followed by red berries in the fall. These berries persist throughout winter unless eaten by birds. Rutgers rating B, rabbit-resistant, full sun or partial sun, Zones 4-7.

Crocus (crocus) (KROH-kus)

Crocus blooms are often the first sign of spring and can be seen popping up through the snow just when you thought winter was going to last forever. Plant them in corners around the outside of the house where they will not be bothered. Warning: squirrels love digging up the newly planted bulbs (actually called corms) and they are quite adept at finding them. They originated in the Alpine areas of Europe and are rated for Zones 3-8. The blooms are generally white or purplish, and the leaves look like grass. About six weeks after blooming, they should be allowed to dry out a bit, which is why I recommend not putting them all over. Otherwise, you would be underwatering something else to avoid overwatering these during dormancy. Rutgers rating B. They rarely get above six inches high or wide but are a very welcome sight in March.

Crown Imperial (fritillaria imperialis 'lutea') (frit-il-AR-ee-uh im-peer-ee-AL-is LOO-tee-uh)

The Crown Imperial lives up to its name. The upward spiky leaves above the downward drooping yellow petals are quite impressive and do resemble a crown. The stalks are four feet high, adding to the wow factor. It blooms in spring/summer and requires full sun or at least partial sun. In northern areas, plant them in full sun. In southern areas, they can tolerate partial sun. Bulbs should be planted sideways to prevent water from collecting in the hollow of the bulb and causing bulb rot. The whole plant smells skunky, which repels deer, rabbits, and humans alike. They do well at the back of a garden where they can get tall and not offend our tender noses. Blooms from other varieties can come in purple, white, orange, and red.

Cypress, Bald (taxodium distichum) (taks-OH-dee-um DIS-tik-um)

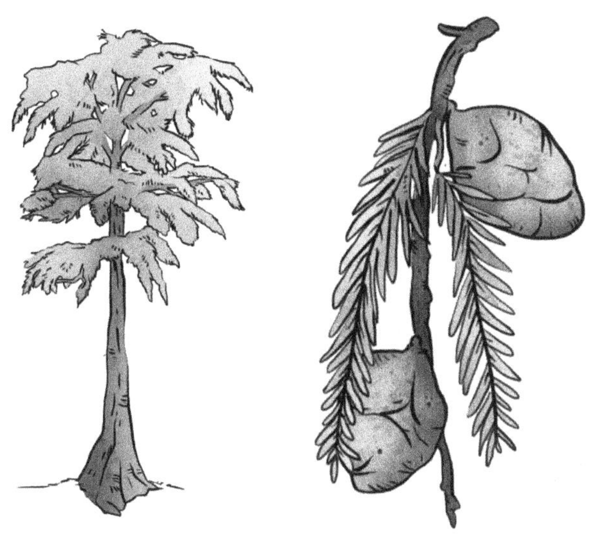

Bald Cypress looks like an Evergreen tree, but its leaves turn coppery-brown and fall off in the fall, thus earning the description Bald. It is found in Zones 4-10 and likes full or partial sun. It even tolerates moist soil and can be found along riverbanks. It is the state tree of Louisiana, and when found in the bayous, it develops knobby 'knees' where the roots take awkward angles. The deer dislike the needles because they tickle the nose. That's my theory, anyway.

Daffodil (narcissus) (nar-SIS-us)

Everyone likes to see the Daffodils rise in early spring, showing us that we have indeed survived another winter. When I lived in Lake Villa, Illinois, someone bequeathed a lot of money to plant daffodils, so you'd see them everywhere. The different varieties have slightly different colors but are basically a wide-petaled flower with a cup in the center, earning them the nickname Buttercup. In Zones 4-8, they thrive in full sun to partial shade and need well-drained soil. They can tolerate drought once established in their dormant season. Plant bulbs four to ten inches apart and at least three inches deep. It may look sparse at first, but they self-multiply, and after a few years you'll have a sea of yellow. The 'actaea' variety is fairly tolerant of wet soils. They are poisonous to most deer, rabbits, and squirrels. They are often planted under trees, where they get enough sun in the spring before the tree's leaves obstruct the sun. Rutgers rating A.

Deutzia (deutzia) (DOOT-zee-uh)

Deutzias are dense shrubs that can be used for an informal hedge. The shrub is covered in tiny white flowers in the spring for two weeks, and the fragrance repels deer but not humans. It is native to Japan but can be grown in Zones 5-8 with full sun or partial sun. It can grow to twenty feet high, but usually only five feet, and spreads to about five feet across. Rutgers rating B.

Devil's Walking Stick (aralia spinosa) (uh-RAY-lee-uh spy-NO-suh)

The Devil's Walking Stick, sometimes called the Hercules Club, gets its name from the spiny thorns on the main trunk. It is native to the eastern US and thrives in Zones 4-9, growing to 15 feet tall in full sun or partial sun. The small white flowers arrive in the summer, giving way to black fruit and yellow to reddish-purple leaves in the fall. Some people get allergic reactions from touching the bark, so be careful pruning. And do prune, as it spreads rapidly. Bees love the flowers, but birds wait for the fruit to nibble on. Rutgers rating A. Other names are Angelica tree and Prickly Ash.

Dogwood, Flowering (cormus) (KOR-mus)

The Flowering Dogwood tree grows fast and spreads fast, so keep an eye on it if you want it confined. In Zones 3-7, it grows to about ten feet tall. Flowers are small and white, followed by white fruit tinged with blue-green, which birds love. Leaves turn bright yellow in full sun but only greenish-yellow in partial shade. Once established, it can tolerate dry soil as well as occasional standing water. Pruning is not required, but many gardeners prune it back about a quarter or even to eight inches off the ground every two to three years to stimulate better color. Rabbit-resistant.

Elder (sambucus) (sam-BYOO-kus)

The Elder, sometimes called Elderberry, is a sprawling shrub that can tolerate wet soils, making it ideal for along rivers. In Zones 3-9, it prefers full sun but can tolerate partial sun. Heavy snow in the winter can damage branches so you may want to prune this shrub severely in the fall. It has the best yellow foliage in full sun. Tiny white lemon-scented flowers appear in early summer, attracting butterflies, giving way to black berries, which birds like and humans can make into elderberry jam. Rutgers rating B. Max height twelve feet and width ten feet. It spreads with suckers, so prune them away if you don't want it to grow out of bounds. Elderberry tea may help reduce a fever. Elder bark tea is a folk remedy for fighting colds and sore throats.

Elm (ulmus) (ULM-us)

The Elm tree was a common sight until Dutch Elm Disease ravaged them. Now some varieties are resistant to that blight. They prefer full sun in Zones 4-9 and have very insignificant green flowers in the spring. In the fall, the seed pods fly away on wings that resemble flying saucers. They commonly reach forty feet high and are fast-growing. Slippery Elm bark tea may relieve a sore throat. Some use it with mint for stomach pain. Traditional herbal medicine sources recommend it for an irritated digestive tract. It is also used to treat asthma. An all-around useful herb, I would say.

Fir, Douglas (pseudotsuga menziesii) (SOO-doh SOO-guh menz-ESS-ee-eye)

The Douglas Fir is one of the largest trees in the world and is native to the Pacific Northwest. It can be grown in Zones 4-6, but I wouldn't recommend it in town as it grows up to eighty feet tall. If left to its own devices, it can grow to three hundred feet tall and doesn't mind higher elevations at all. It does not like drought or hot summers. It requires full sun. Deer don't like the prickly branches or their aroma when touched. Rutgers rating B.

Flower, Blanket (gaillardia) (gay-LAR-dee-uh)

The Blanket Flower is native to the northwestern US but will do well in Zones 3-10. The origin of its name is controversial. Some say it refers to the yellow, orange, and red colors of the flowers being similar to the colors found in Native American blankets. Others say it is because the blooms will blanket the ground. It is happiest in full sun and will reach three feet high. The flowers bloom from spring to fall, attracting butterflies. The tiny berries that follow the blooms attract birds, especially Goldfinches. It prefers moist, well-drained soils but will tolerate drought conditions. It will not tolerate clay soils.

Forsythia, Northern Sun (forsythia x intermedia) (for-SITH-ee-a ex in-ter-MEE-dee-uh)

The Northern Sun Forsythia is often the first bloom in the spring, the yellow flowers reminding you that winter will not last forever. The flower buds are in by mid-July, so don't prune after that or you'll kill the flowers for next year. They will not always flower well in Zone 5, as the flower buds will die if the temperature hits five below zero. Since they can spread widely, pruning back to almost ground level every four to five years is recommended. This plant isn't picky when it comes to other conditions. It will grow in full sun to partial sun, although the flowers will be less showy in partial sun. It tolerates poor soils and even drought once established. Rated for Zones 5-8, it grows to about six feet high and just as wide. Rutgers rating B.

Fothergilla (fothergilla) (foth-er-GIL-la)

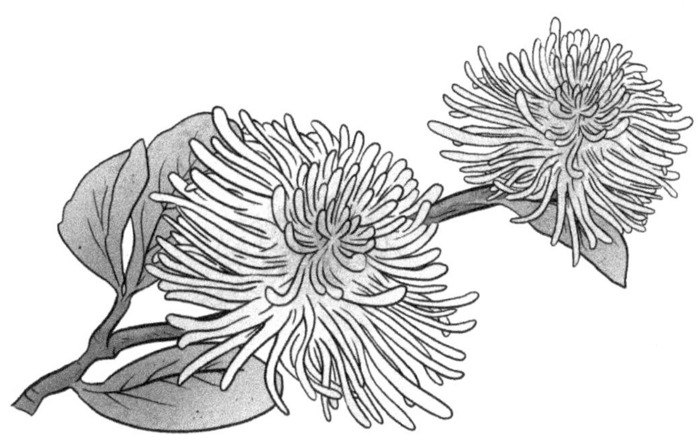

Fothergillas are shrubs native to the southeastern US but can live in Zones 4-8. It prefers acidic soil, as do Rhododendrons, so you can plant them nearby. Its white, fragrant spring flowers resemble bottle brushes, which is why deer dislike them. It slowly reaches six feet in height and the same in width. It thrives in full sun but can tolerate partial sun or even shade. Rutgers rating B. Leaves turn yellow, orange, and even reddish-purple in the fall.

Ginkgo (ginkgo biloba) (GING-ko bi-LOW-buh)

Ginkgo trees were a favorite of Frank Lloyd Wright in his landscaping designs, and I often drove past them in Oak Park, Illinois on my way to work. They turn yellow in the fall. Make sure you only plant male trees, as the female trees produce fruit that smells awful when they ripen and split. Ginkgos are considered the only surviving tree that was on Earth 150 million years ago. It will reach a hundred feet tall if left alone. It requires full sun and thrives in Zones 4-9. The spring blooms are green, so they are hard to spot. It is tolerant of salt, making it good along a road. They are also called Maidenhair trees. Tea made from the leaves may be used as a remedy for all sorts of ailments as it is said to improve circulation.

Glory-of-the-Snow (chionodoxa luciliae) (kye-oh-no-DOKS-uh luh-SIL-ee-ay)

As you might suspect from the name, Glory of the Snow emerges in early spring when there is some snow left on the ground, and mixes well with other early bloomers such as Tulips, Daffodils, and Snowdrops. Plant bulbs about three inches deep and three inches apart in the fall and they will naturalize to form a carpet of blooms. You can plant them under deciduous trees, as they are already dormant when the tree's leaves appear. They are native to western Turkey and can be grown in Zones 3-8. Flowers can be blue, pink, or white.

Golddust (aucuba japonica) (AWK-yoo-bah juh-PON-ih-kuh)

Golddust, also called Spotted Laurel, is native to China's riverbanks and can be grown in Zones 6-10. It prefers partial sun or full shade, and can reach ten feet in height and six feet in spread. The white blooms arrive in spring, slightly larger on the male plant. Be sure you plant male and female plants together if you want berries. Protect it from wind, especially in northern Zones. If you are north of Zone 6, put it in a container and bring it in for the winter. It likes winter temperatures of 50-65 degrees, so don't put it in the den. You can grow it as a houseplant as well, and it will keep its leaves year-round. It is drought-resistant and has a Rutgers rating of B.

Hawthorn, English (formerly crataegus laevigata, now crataegus rhytidophylla) (krah-TEE-gus ry-ti-do-FIL-uh)

We treasure English Hawthorn trees for their prolific white blooms in the spring, but deer don't like the thorns. Nobody does, which explains their widespread use in England in the 1800s as a hedge. They are also susceptible to many diseases and pests. In Zones 4-7 they can grow to twenty feet high with a spread just as wide, making them good shade trees. They do better in colder areas where the pests can't get such a stranglehold. Birds love the berries, which are also edible for humans. Butterflies love the blossoms. They do best in full sun and medium moisture soil. Rutgers rating B. Hawthorn extract is said to improve circulation and is considered by some to be good for throat problems.

Hazelnut (corylus americana) (KOR-ih-lus a-mer-ih-KAH-na)

The Hazelnut tree, also called a Filbert tree, is a shrub that can grow up to sixteen feet tall with a twelve-foot spread. A native American, it grows in Zones 3-9 in full sun or partial sun. There are separate male and female flowers on each plant, the male being more showy in yellowish-brown catkins, the female being smaller in red, inconspicuous catkins. Female flowers give way to nuts, which can be eaten or ground into flour but are usually left for the birds. The fall color depends on the variety. It is susceptible to Eastern Filbert Blight and is tolerant of clay soils. Rutgers rating B.

Holly (ilex) (EYE-leks)

Holly reminds me of Christmas with its green leaves and red berries. If you want berries, make sure to plant both male and female plants. The serrated leaf edges irritate deer. The flowers arrive in spring, followed by berries in the fall. The berries remain throughout the winter if the birds don't gobble them up. Rated for Zones 3-10, it can reach twenty feet tall and likes full sun and partial sun. It appreciates the partial shade in hot summers and needs well-drained soil.

Hop Tree (ptelea trifoliata) (TEL-ee-uh try-foh-lee-AT-uh)

The Hop Tree is native to the eastern and midwestern US, and the seeds were used as Hop substitutes when making beer in colonial times. The unpleasant smell of its bark and leaves when bruised and flowers give it another nickname- Stinking Ash. It is easily grown in well-drained dry to medium soils in the shade and partial sun. It will tolerate full sun but does not prefer it. Rated for Zones 4-9, it is adaptable to a wide variety of growing conditions, and the smell keeps the deer away. The greenish-white flowers in the spring give way to seeds having a flat area all around, similar to Ash trees. It can grow to twenty feet high and to a spread of twenty feet as well.

Hyacinth (hyacinthus) (hy-uh-SIN-thus)

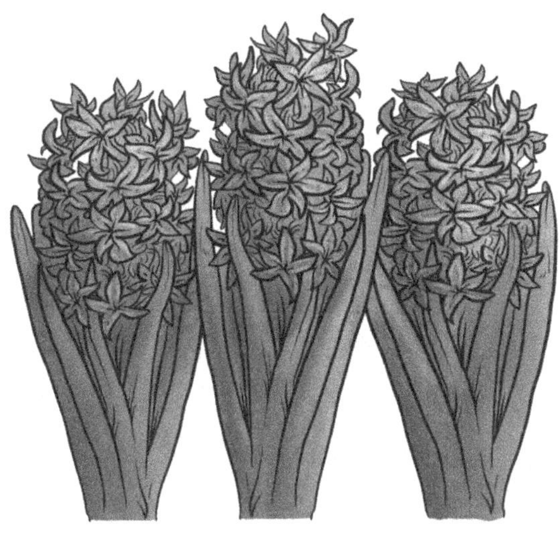

Hyacinths are famous for their flowers, which form spikes surrounded by blooms and are almost overpowering in their scent. The bulbs often decrease in the ability to bloom after the first year, so should be replaced every year or two. Bulbs can also be forced in pots for winter bloom. Wear gloves when handling the bulbs to avoid allergic reactions. The flowers come in a rainbow of colors: blue, purple, white, pink, red, and variegated or plain. Rated for Zones 4-9, they will grow in full or partial sun and medium well-drained soil. Plant in fall four to six inches apart. Plant about a dozen for the best effect. Keep the soil moist at first to encourage root growth, then taper off. Keep soil moist during bloom, then taper off as the plant goes dormant. The plants are small, only a foot tall, and half a foot wide. Rabbit-resistant and Rutgers rating B.

Hyacinth, Grape (muscari) (mus-KAR-ee)

Grape Hyacinths are similar to regular Hyacinths, but the bloom clusters are narrower. Rated for Zones 4-8, they reach only nine inches tall and six inches wide. Leaves come up in the fall to survive the winter, followed by spikes of flowers in the early spring in blue, purple, white, or yellow, adding a splash of color to an otherwise drab landscape. It likes full sun or partial sun and medium soil. It will tolerate clay soil. These bulbs can also be forced in pots for winter blooming. Rutgers rating B.

Ironwood (ostrya virginiana) (OSS-tree-uh vir-jin-ee-AN-uh)

Ironwood trees, also known as Eastern Hop Hornbeam trees, are native to the Midwest down to Mexico, Zones 3-9. It will grow to twenty-five feet tall by twenty feet wide in full sun to part sun, with medium moisture soil. A low maintenance plant, it is popular for use as a street tree or shade tree. The flowers are easy to miss- reddish-brown male blooms and light green female blooms that appear on separate catkins on the same tree. The female catkins are followed by drooping clusters of sac-like seed-bearing pods which resemble hops. The leaves turn a dull yellow in the fall and often drop early.

Iris (iris) (EYE-ris)

Iris blooms remind me of Easter. They bloom in the late spring in Zones 3-10, like full sun but will tolerate partial sun, especially in the hot afternoon. The flowers are available in many colors, but the most common one is white. Water them consistently until after blooming ends. They do best in sandy ground with good drainage. When they get overcrowded, divide them and replant. Plant shallowly with a third of the plant above the soil and the roots spread out for support. They usually reach about three feet tall. You can plant these in the spring or the fall, but plants that have the winter to grow deep roots have a better chance of blooming next year.

Juniper, Chinese (juniperus chinensis) (jew-NIP-er-us chi-NEN-sis)

The Chinese Juniper is usually grown as a tree, reaching fifty feet high with a thirty-foot spread, but it can also be grown as a shrub. Native to China (you guessed that from the title), it is rated for Zones 4-9 and has a Rutgers rating of B. It needs full sun and well-drained soil and is not tolerant of clay or wet soils. Male plants produce Catkin-like pollen cones. Female plants produce seed-bearing cones that take two years to mature.

Juniper, Common (juniperus communis) (jew-NIP-er-us KOM-yoo-nis)

The Common Juniper is a true Northerner, rated for Zones 2-6. Depending on your latitude, it can be a low groundcover or a shrub reaching fifteen feet high by twelve feet wide. It grows best in full sun with medium moisture, well-drained soil, and has good drought tolerance once established. It can also do well in rocky or dry soil. Plant male and female plants together to get berries, which take two to three years to ripen and are used to flavor gin. They are tolerant of salt, so you can plant them along the road if you wish. According to tradition, Juniper berries are said to relieve symptoms of urinary tract infections.

Kerria, Japanese (kerria japonica) (KER-ee-a juh-PON-ih-kuh)

Japanese Kerria is sometimes called the Easter Rose because the profuse yellow blooms arrive around Easter and the flowers resemble roses. Rated for Zones 4-9, it prefers partial sun to shade. The flowers can fade if exposed to too much sun. This shrub can grow to five feet tall by eight feet wide. Prune back after flowering, as the flowers grow on last year's growth. It doesn't like heavy clay soils but is tolerant of both dry and wet soil.

Larch (larix) (LAR-iks)

The Larch tree needs a lot of room to grow, reaching a hundred feet tall and thirty feet wide. It likes cool summers and cold winters and is rated for Zone 2-6. Its needles make you think it's an evergreen, but they turn yellow in the fall and drop. It prefers moist, gravelly loams and will not tolerate dry soil or city pollution. Rutgers rating A.

Laurel, Drooping (leucothoe fontanesiana) (loo-KOH-thoh-ee fon-tay-nee-zee-AH-na)

The Drooping Laurel is an evergreen bush native to the eastern US from New York south along the Appalachians. It grows best in moist, acidic, organically rich, cool, well-drained soils in partial shade. It can be grown in full sun if you water it consistently. It does not tolerate drought or high winds. It can also be grown in full shade. Rated for Zones 5-8, mulch it well and plant it in a protected location. The white flowers appear in May, and eventually, the plant will reach three feet high by three feet wide.

Laurel, Mountain (kalmia) (KAL-mee-uh)

Mountain Laurel can be grown in Zones 4-9 in cool, moist, acidic, well-drained soil. Mulch to keep roots cool and retain moisture. It can tolerate a wide variety of sunlight levels but does best in partial sun, having some morning light and afternoon shade. The flowers are rose to white with purple markings and arrive in late spring in a spectacular display. It grows into a dense shrub about fifteen feet high, growing gnarly with age. The leaves are leathery and glossy, which explains the plant's deer-resistant and rabbit-resistant ratings.

Lilac, Common (syringa vulgaris) (si-RING-gah vul-GAIR-iss)

One of my neighbors growing up had a Lilac bush. I used to detour to walk past it when it was blooming and pause to absorb the aroma. Lilacs can be found in Zones 3-7 and can grow to sixteen feet high with a twelve foot spread. The May blooms arrive in large clumps, like Hyacinths, and hummingbirds and butterflies love them. It can survive partial sun with fewer blooms, but it performs best in full sun. Rutgers rating B and rabbit-resistant.

Lily, Turf (liriope spicata) (lir-RYE-oh-pee spi-KAH-tuh)

The Turf Lily, also called Creeping Liriope, is a ground cover that reaches eighteen inches in height and twelve inches in spread, flowering in tiny, lavender to white blooms in the summer. It is in the Asparagus family, can spread aggressively, and should be mowed in the spring. It can help stabilize a slope. It prefers moist, well-drained soil in full sun to partial sun. Rutgers rating B and rabbit-resistant. Once established, it is drought-resistant as well. Zones 4-10.

Maple, Full Moon (acer japonicum o-isami) (AY-ser juh-PON-ih-kum oh ih-SAH-mee)

Maple trees are a little confusing when it comes to deer-resistance. Rutgers gives the species as a whole a B rating, but Missouri Botanical Garden doesn't list deer-resistance on any of the numerous Maple trees. The variety acer japonicum o-isami or Full Moon Maple is rabbit-resistant. Maple trees as a whole have yellow to red coloring in the fall, making them stand out from other trees and making them my favorite. The small flowers arrive in the spring, followed by "helicopter seeds," officially known as winged samaras, which take the seeds far and wide. They can grow in full sun or partial sun, and the different varieties range from an eight foot tall shrub to a fifty foot tall tree. They can be grown in Zones 3-9 and are fairly drought-resistant once established.

Myrtle, Crape (lagerstroemia indica) (la-ger-STREEM-ee-a IN-dih-kuh)

Crape Myrtle is a shrub native to Asia that grows in Zones 6-9 in full sun. The red, pink, or white flowers show up in the summer. It can reach twenty-five feet high with a spread of twenty feet in the southern US, but only about ten feet in the Midwest. Plant in protected areas and apply mulch in winter as they are prone to die back almost to the ground, depending on the severity of the winter. Rutgers rating B.

Nannyberry (viburnum lentago) (vy-BUR-num lent-AH-go)

Nannyberry plants are multi-stemmed shrubs that can also be trained to be single-stemmed trees. They grow in Zones 2-8 in full sun to partial sun in average, well-drained soils. Prune directly after flowering because buds form in summer for the following year. White flowers appear in the spring, giving way to blue-black berries in the fall that persist through the winter if the birds don't eat them up. These berries are edible and can be eaten off the plant or made into jams and preserves. Nanny goats are reported to have eaten the berries more than billy goats, which somehow caused the name. Once established, it resists drought and heat. The plants can reach sixteen feet tall in ideal conditions. Note that this is a subspecies of Viburnum, mentioned later.

Oak (quercus) (KWER-kus)

The Oak Tree does not have any aromatic flowers to drive the deer away. It simply is better at resisting the damage that deer inflict by rubbing their antlers against the bark. Grown all over America in Zones 3-8, it grows best in rich, acidic soil in full sun. It can tolerate clay soils and dry soils. It slowly grows to eighty feet tall and even one hundred feet tall in the wild. Make sure it has plenty of room to spread out to about eighty feet wide. Of course, it grows slowly, making it less popular among many gardeners. If you plant one today in your twenties, your grandchildren will enjoy it at full size. It also tends to outcompete other trees for the sun and can stump the growth of other trees by denying them light. The acidity of the soil around an Oak tree can damage other plants also.

Orange, Mock (philadelphus) (fil-uh-DEL-fuss)

Mock Orange shrubs are named because the late spring flowers reminded someone of Orange blossoms. Rated for Zones 3-8, it can not tolerate wet soil but does best in moist, well-drained soil and full sun or partial sun. Prune directly after the flowers fade, as next year's flowers grow on this year's growth. It may be pruned to the ground if it becomes scraggly. Usually grows to about four feet high and as wide.

PawPaw (asimina triloba) (a-SEE-mee-nuh try-LO-buh)

PawPaw plants are small trees or large shrubs, depending on who you talk to, reaching thirty feet in height and width. They prefer full sun or partial sun and medium to wet soil and are found in Zones 5-9. The fragrant purple flowers arrive in late spring, followed by fruit, which is edible and used in ice cream and pie. Some people don't like them as they can upset their stomachs, but most people in the south look forward to eating them if they beat the wildlife (raccoons, squirrels, and opossums) to them. Plant two of them to get fruit. They spread by root suckers to form hedges and thickets. Rutgers rating A.

Pine, Scotch (pinus sylvestris) (PY-nus sil-VESS-triss)

Scotch Pines are the only Pine trees native to Great Britain and are rated for Zones 2-9. They grow to sixty feet tall commonly and can reach one hundred and fifty feet in the wild. They need full sun and like acidic, well-drained soil. They are a Christmas tree favorite. Once established, they can tolerate poor soils, even clay or sandy soils, as long as the drainage is good. They are distinctive in the following ways: twisted, blue-green needles up to three inches long in bundles of two; gray to light brown cones up to three inches long; and scaly, orange-red bark near the top but darker reddish-brown near the base. They prefer cool summers. Rutgers rating B.

Redbud, Eastern (cercis canadensis) (SER-sis ka-na-DEN-sis)

The Eastern Redbud tree is native to Eastern and Central North America and is the state tree of Oklahoma. It ranges from Canada to Texas in Zones 4-8 where it prefers full sun, although welcomes some afternoon shade in the South. The multi-trunk style makes it look more like a shrub than a tree. The tree doesn't like to be transplanted, so pick your site carefully. The rose-purple flowers arrive in April, on bare branches followed by seed pods that can remain on the tree all winter. The leaves can be blue-green or dark green, which may explain the deer's dislike. Butterflies love them. Under ideal conditions it can reach twenty feet high and a little wider than it is tall.

Redwood, Dawn (metasequoia glyptostroboides) (met-uh-see-KWOY-uh glip-toh-stroh-BOY-deez)

Dawn Redwood trees are deciduous, coniferous, and can grow up to a hundred feet tall. The fossil record shows that they existed fifty million years ago, but it wasn't until 1941 that any live trees were discovered in China. As the tree grows, the trunk develops elaborate fluting, which deepens into fissures as the tree ages. The foliage is fern-like, feathery, and soft to the touch. Best grown in humus-rich, medium to wet, well-drained soil in full sun, it requires a lot of room to grow. Zones 4-8, Rutgers rating B.

Rhododendron (rhododendron) (roh-do-DEN-dron)

The Rhododendron genus includes about 900 species of both Rhododendrons and Azaleas, both evergreen and deciduous. They originate in the northern hemisphere and are grown for their showy white, pink, red, or purple spring flowers and, if evergreen, their winter foliage. True Rhododendrons have ten stamens in a flower, and Azaleas have only five. Most are rated for Zones 3-9 and grow to be about six feet tall and wide. They require full sun to partial sun and medium moisture, well-drained soil. Plant in an area protected from high winds and far from trees in the Walnut family (Walnuts, Butternuts, Pecans, and Hickories). Shallow root systems will benefit from mulching and require pH from 5.0 to 5.5 to thrive. Do not cultivate near roots and do not let them dry out. These plants are susceptible to many insect and disease problems. Rabbit-resistant. Rhododendron tea may be taken to allieve arthritic pain according to herbal medicine lore.

Rose of Sharon (hibiscus syriacus) (hi-BIS-kus seer-ee-AK-us)

The Rose of Sharon shrub grows to twelve feet high by ten feet wide with abundant white to pink flowers from June to October in Zones 5-8. Native to China, it needs full sun to partial sun and medium moisture, well-drained soil. It can tolerate poor soil and some drought once established. Easily propagated from stem cuttings or seeds, but seeds may not have the same flower color as the parent. It can self-seed rather aggressively under optimum growing conditions, so keep an eye on it. Rutgers rating B.

Sassafras (sassafras albidum) (SASS-uh-frass AL-bi-dum)

The Sassafras tree is native to Eastern North America and does well in Zones 4-9 in medium soil and full or part sun. It prefers acidic soil but can tolerate a range of soil types, as long as you don't mind the leaves turning yellow in alkaline soils. It spreads by root suckers, so keep it in check or it will end up looking more like a shrub than a tree. It forms a pyramidal shape about thirty feet tall. The large taproot makes transplanting difficult. Greenish-yellow flowers on female trees produce grape-like clusters in September if pollinated. Excellent red, yellow, and purple fall leaf color. Native Americans used the tree for many culinary uses, and some sources suggest Sassafras tea for preventing breast cancer, but the FDA has recently found carcinogens in the oils, so I wouldn't suggest making any tea.

Serviceberry, Allegheny (amelanchier laevis) (am-uh-LAN-kee-er LAY-viss)

Allegheny Serviceberry trees can be grown in Zones 4-8 in full sun to partial sun. It is tolerant of a wide range of soils but prefers moist, well-drained loams. It usually grows to ten to fifteen feet tall, so can be considered a short tree or tall shrub, depending on who you talk to. White, fairly fragrant, drooping flowers appear in April, followed by berries in June, giving it an alternate name of Juneberry. Native to Eastern North America. The berries are often used in jams, jellies, and pies, and resemble blueberries in appearance and taste. Rutgers rating B.

Smoketree (cotinus coggygria) (ko-TYE-nus kog-GY-gree-uh)

The Smoketree or Smokebush is a shrub native to central Asia and Europe. It grows in Zones 5-8 in full sun. Due to a shallow root system it can't tolerate wet, poorly drained soils. It grows in dry, rocky soil where many other plants have problems. It reaches ten to fifteen feet high and as wide. It gets its name from the billowy hairs which grow on the spent flower clusters. These hairs stay all summer and turn the shrub into a smoky-pink to purplish-pink cloud, and may explain why the deer don't like them very much. I think they tickle their noses. The blue-green leaves turn attractive colors in the fall.

Snowdrops (galanthus nivalis) (guh-LAN-thus niv-VAL-us)

Snowdrops grow in Zones 3-7 and are often the first flower to bloom, arriving in February. They are small, only nine inches high and six inches wide. They prefer full sun or partial sun but could be planted under deciduous trees since the trees have no leaves at the time. Plant bulbs two to three inches apart and two to three inches deep in large groups of two dozen or more for the best effect. In ideal conditions, the bulbs will self-seed. Allow the leaves to yellow before removing the bulb from the ground. You don't have to remove the bulb at all if you don't need to replant it elsewhere. It will go dormant once done blooming. Blooms are white and droopy. Rutgers rating A.

Sourwood (oxydendrum arboreum) (oks-ee-DEN-drum ar-BOR-ee-um)

The Sourwood or Sorrell tree is native to the Eastern US and does best in full sun and acidic soils in Zones 5-9. It pairs well with other acidic soil-loving varities in the Heath family such as azaleas and rhododendrons. It generally grows to thirty feet high by fifteen feet wide and does not do well with drought or urban conditions. Waxy, white flowers arrive in early summer, followed by dry capsules that open to silver-gray in the fall. This gives a pleasant contrast with the crimson red fall coloring of the leaves. The flowers are slightly aromatic; combine that with the gray bark and gray seeds and the deer prefer to pass by. Bees are fond of the flowers and many people are fond of their honey.

Spruce, Norway (picea) (PY-see-uh)

Norway Spruce trees grow fast and reach sixty feet tall by thirty feet wide in Zones 2-8. They like their summers cool but sunny as they require full sun. They prefer acidic, rich soils but tolerate sandy soils well and dryish soils once established. They don't flower but produce large cones about nine inches long that hang down from the branches. They're handy as windbreaks, and dwarf varieties are available for gardens.

Squill, Siberian (scilla siberica) (SIL-uh sy-BEER-ah-kuh)

Siberian Squill loves northern Minnesota and Michigan's upper peninsula as the seasons remind it of home in Siberia. It is rated for Zones 2-11 with full sun or partial sun. It only gets six inches high, but the blue flowers in spring are beautiful. these bulbs are planted in fall about three inches deep, and they will spread by both bulb offshoots and self-seeding. Plant these around trees and shrubs or in sweeping drifts on slopes or along shady river banks. Rutgers rating A. VERY poisonous when ingested, so don't plant around young children or pets. Can irritate skin in susceptible people.

Sumac, Fragrant (rhus aromatica) (roos ar-oh-MAT-ih-kuh)

Fragrant Sumac is a shrub with smaller leaves similar to Poison Sumac, but this plant is not poisonous. The leaves and twigs are aromatic when bruised, giving rise to the name. It grows in Zones 3-9 to a height of six feet and a width of ten feet. The leaves turn attractive colors in the fall. It spreads quickly to form a thicket. The shrubs grow in full sun or partial sun and in a wide range of soils as long as they are well-drained. Tiny yellow flowers bloom in April and give way to berries on the female plant. Sometimes there are both male and female on the same plant, but usually they are separate. Birds love the berries. Rutgers rating A and rabbit-resistant.

Summersweet (clethra alnifolia) (KLEE-thra al-nee-FOH-lee-uh)

Summersweet, also called Sweet Pepperbush, is a popular shrub because it can bloom in partial shade in the late summer. In Zones 3-9, it can grow to eight feet tall by six feet wide in full sun to partial sun and consistently moist, acidic, sandy soils. It prefers partial shade and tolerates clay soils and full shade, but the soil should not be allowed to dry out. The leaves turn nice colors in the fall. The white flowers are aromatic and very attractive to butterflies and bees.

Sweet-Gum (liquidambar styraciflua) (lih-kwid-AM-bar sty-rak-ee-FLOO-uh)

The Sweet-Gum tree can be grown in Zones 5-9 in full sun and medium moisture, well-drained soil. It can tolerate poor soils but not anything less than full sun. The yellow-green flowers emerge in the spring and give way to fruit clusters that harden in the fall and stay on the tree until late winter. Don't plant this tree near a walkway as those hard clusters can trip you up as they fall during the winter. The sap is gummy and used in several applications such as chewing gum, incense, perfumes, folk medicines, and flavorings. The wood is used for furniture, home interiors, and flooring. The leaves are fragrant when bruised and turn wonderful colors in the fall. In ideal conditions, this tree can reach eighty feet tall. Rabbit-resistant.

Sweet-Spire, Virginia (itea virginica) (eye-TEE-uh vir-JIN-ih-kuh)

Virginia Sweet-Spire is a native American that grows to five feet tall and five feet wide in Zones 5-9, in full sun or partial sun, and in medium to wet soil. It can form dense colonies by root suckering if left unchecked. White flowers cover the shrub in late spring to early summer. The leaves turn red, orange, and gold shades in fall and often take their time falling to the ground. Rutgers rating B.

Sycamore, American (platanus occidentalis) (PLAT-an-us ok-sih-den-TAY-liss)

The American Sycamore tree is enormous. It can grow to one hundred feet high and one hundred feet wide with a huge trunk measuring up to eight feet across. It is the most massive tree in America and needs a large space. It is also a litterbug, dropping twigs, leaves, fruiting balls, and bark. A sign of a Sycamore you can spot from afar is the exfoliating trunk. Brown bark comes off to reveal the white inner bark. Spring flowers are yellow for males and red for females. Female flowers give way to fruiting balls that eventually burst, dispersing seeds on downy tufts. The wood is used for furniture, crates, barrels, and butcher blocks. Native Americans hollowed out the trunks for canoes. It grows in Zones 4-9 in medium to wet soils in full sun. Also known as Sycamore, Eastern Sycamore, Buttonwood, or Buttonball trees, it can be found in the wild along riverbanks. It will tolerate light shade.

Tree, Chinese Fringe (chionanthus retusus) (kye-oh-NAN-thus re-TOO-sus)

The Chinese Fringe Tree is spectacular in spring when the white flowers bloom. They seem to cover every inch of the tree. It can be grown in Zones 5-9 in medium well-drained soil in full sun or partial sun, although the best flowering occurs with full sun. It can reach twenty feet high with a spread just as large. It prefers acidic soils and can not tolerate prolonged dry conditions. There are separate male and female plants, although they might not be properly labeled. If fertilized, the female flowers give way to olive-like fruits that ripen to bluish-black and feed wildlife during the winter. Leaves turn yellow in the fall. Exfoliating gray-brown bark is attractive in the winter. Rutgers rating B.

Tree, Katsura (cercidiphyllum japonicum) (ser-sid-ih-FIL-um juh-PON-ih-kum)

The Katsura Tree can be grown in Zones 4-8 in rich, moist, well-drained soil in full sun or partial sun. Not tolerant of drought, especially when young, it grows best in an area protected from strong winds and hot afternoon sun. There are separate male and female trees, with slightly different but unimpressive flowers. Clusters of greenish pods follow pollinated flowers on female trees. Leaves turn a spectacular range of red, orange, and gold in the fall, and smell like cinnamon or apples. Trees can reach sixty feet high and just as wide and are good selections for shade trees. Rutgers rating A.

Tree, Tulip (liriodendron tulipifera) (ly-ree-oh-DEN-dron too-lip-EE-fer-uh)

The Tulip Tree, also known as the Yellow Poplar, is the state tree of Indiana, Kentucky, and Tennessee. Its wood is used for furniture, plywood, boatbuilding, paper pulp, and general lumber. Native Americans used the hollowed-out trunks for canoes. The cup-like flowers bloom in the spring and are yellow with an orange band at the base of each petal. Even though the flowers are two inches long, they can often go unnoticed because they arrive after the leaves fully form. Winged seeds follow the flowers. It is best grown in organically rich, well-drained soil in full sun. It will tolerate partial sun. Rated for Zones 4-9, it grows to ninety feet tall with a fifty foot spread. It has impressive fall color and is rabbit-resistant. Rutgers rating B.

Viburnum (viburnum) (vy-BUR-num)

Viburnum is a somewhat early bloomer, arriving in March or April. Plant these in a protected location to prevent losing these flowers to hard freezes. It can be grown in Zones 2-10 in medium moisture, well-drained soils in full sun or partial sun, although you'll get better flowers in full sun. Avoid soils that are either too dry or too wet, as it is a bit picky. The fragrant, tubular flowers bloom on bare stems. These flowers are replaced in late summer by red berries that become blackish in the late fall. The shrub can grow to ten feet high and six feet wide. Plant it where you can enjoy the early fragrant flowers to the utmost. Rutgers rating A. Viburnum opulus teas are considered helpful pain relievers, especially menstrual cramps, according to herbal medicine sources.

Weigela (weigela florida) (wy-GEE-la FLOR-id-uh)

Weigela is a dense shrub that grows to ten feet tall and twelve feet wide in full sun in Zones 4-9. In southern areas, it may appreciate some light dappled shade in the afternoon. The pink flowers explode from April to June, with some sporadic reblooming later. Hummingbirds and humans alike love these flowers. It can tolerate clay soil. Rutgers rating B.

Witchhazel, Common (hamamelis) (ham-uh-MEE-lis)

Common Witchhazel is a shrub grown in Zones 3-9 in moist, acidic, well-drained soil in full sun to partial sun. The odd-looking, spiky, reddish-purple flowers herald the approach of spring with their arrival in February or March, with the best flowering occurring in full sun. It can tolerate clay soil as long as the drainage is good. The leaves turn a showy yellow in the fall. Root suckers propagate it, so be sure to remove them as you see them. Prune after flowering. It can reach nine feet in height. Rutgers rating B. Witchhazel can be used on the skin as an astringent in traditional herbal medicine.

Yew, Japanese Plum (cephalotaxus harringtonia) (sef-uh-loh-TAKS-us har-ring-TOH-nee-uh)

Japanese Plum Yew is a needled evergreen that does well in partial sun and full shade in moist, sandy, well-drained soils. It will tolerate full sun in cool northern summers, but prefers afternoon shade in areas with hot summers. I would plant it in a shady location, as our summers can become hot. Rated for Zones 4-9, it reaches ten feet in any direction but grows slowly. In Zones 4 and 5, plant them in sheltered locations for winter survival. Both male and female plants are needed for fruit production. The fruit resembles plums and is edible. The rest of the plant is toxic, so I'm not sure I would chance the fruit. Rutgers rating A.

Chapter Six

Invasive and Poisonous Plants

Some plants are deer-resistant but are also considered invasive weeds in the Midwest or surrounding areas, so don't even think about planting them. Note that this list includes both Spring and Fall plants. These include:

- Akebia (akebia quinata) (a-KEE-bee-uh kwi-NAY-tuh)

- Sweet Alyssum (lobularia maritima) (lob-yoo-LAR-ee-uh mar-ih-TEE-muh)

- Baby's Breath (gypsophila paniculata) (jip-SOF-il-uh pan-ick-yoo-LAH-tuh)

- Bachelor's Button (centaurea cyanus) (sen-TAR-ee-uh SY-an-us)

- Bamboo, Yellow Grove or Bamboo, Golden (phyllostachys) (fy-lo-STAK-iss)

- Barberry, Japanese (berberis thunbergii) (BUR-bur-is thun-BERG-ee-eye), also called Oregon Grape-Holly (mahonia japonica) (ma-HO-nee-uh juh-PON-ih-kuh)

- Bishop's Weed (aegopodium podagraria) (ee-guh-POH-dee-um pod-uh-GRAR-ee-uh)

- Buckthorn, Common (rhamnus) (RAM-nus)

- Bugloss (anchusa) (an-KOO-suh)

- Catalpa (catalpa) (kuh-TAL-puh)

- Chocolate Vine (akebia) (a-KEE-bee-uh)

- Forget-Me-Not, Woodland (myosotis sylvatica) (my-oh-SO-tis sil-VAT-ee-kuh)

- Grape-Holly, Oregon (mahonia aquifolium) (ma-HO-nee-uh a-kwee-FOH-lee-um)

- Grass, Ribbon (phalaris arundinacea) (FAL-ah-ris a-run-din-uh-SEE-uh), also called Grass, Red Canary

- Not all of the plants in the miscanthus species are invasive, but the only one that is deer-resistant is Grass, Chinese Silver (miscanthus sinensis) (miss-KANTH-us sy-NEN-sis), which is invasive in Indiana.

- Locust, Black Tree (robinia pseudoacacia) (roh-BIN-ee-uh soo-doh-uh-KAY-see-uh)

- Locust, Honey Tree (gleditsia triacanthus) (gleh-DIT-see-uh try-a-KAN-thus)

- Periwinkle (vinca minor) (VIN-kuh MY-nor)

- Many varieties of Privet (ligustrum) (lig-GUS-trum) are invasive, so steer clear of any of them.

- Sunflower, Common (helianthus annuus) (hee-lee-AN-thus AN-yoo-us)

- Valerian (valeriana officianalis) (va-ler-ee-AH-nuh oh-fiss-ih-NAH-liss), also called heliotrope (hee-lee-oh-TROPE)

- Chinese Wisteria (wisteria sinensis) (wis-TEER-ee-uh sy-NEN-sis)

- Some varieties of Wormwood (artemisia) (ar-the-MEEZ-ee-uh)

The following have been declared invasive in the southeastern US, so I wouldn't recommend planting them. With global warming, they could easily become invasive in the Midwest.

- Elephant Ears (colocasia esculenta) (kol-oh-KAY-see-uh es-kew-LEN-tuh)

- Japanese Blood Grass (imperata cylindrica) (im-per-AH-tuh sil-IN-dree-kuh)

- Turf Lily (liriope spicata) (lir-RYE-oh-pee spi-KAH-tuh)

These plants have not been declared invasive, but are very aggressive spreaders. Plant them in a contained area or keep an eye on them to prevent them from taking over the yard.

- Aster, False (boltonia asteroides) (bol-TO-nee-uh ass-ter-OY-dees)

- Catnip (nepeta cataria) (NEP-eh-tuh kat-AR-ee-uh)

- Chives, Garlic (allium tuberosum) (AL-ee-um too-ber-OH-sum)

- Comfrey (symphytum rubrum) (sim-FY-tum ROO-brum)

- Creeper, Trumpet (campsis radicans) (KAMP-sis RAD-ee-kans)

- Foxglove (digitalis purpurea) (dij-ee-TAH-liss pur-PUR-ee-uh)

- Goldenrod (solidago hybrids) (so-li-DAY-go)

- Horehound (marrubium vulgare) (ma-ROO-bee-um vul-GAIR-ee)

- Horseradish (armoracia rusticana) (ar-mor-AY-shee-uh rus-tik-AH-nuh)

- Jacob's Ladder (polemonium caeruleum) (po-le-MOH-nee-um see-ROO-lee-um)

- Lady's Mantle (alchemilla mollis) (al-kem-ILL-uh MAW-liss)

- Mint, Mountain (pycanthemum pilosum) (pik-NAN-thee-mum pil-OH-sum)

- Morning Glory (ipomea sp) (ip-oh-MEE-a)

- Mullein (verbascum sp) (ver-BASK-um)

- Pennyroyal (mentha pulegium) (Men-thuh pul-ee-GEE-um)

- Plant, Obedient (physostegia virginiana) (fy-so-STEG-ee-uh vir-jin-ee-AN-uh)

- Poppy, Plume (macleaya cordata) (ma-KLAY-uh kor-DAY-tuh)

- St. John's Wort (hypericum calycinum) (hy-PER-ee-kum ka-LEE-kin-um)

- Snow-in-Summer (cerastium tomentosum) (ker-RAS-tee-um toh-men-TOH-sum)

- Violet (viola sp) (vee-OH-la)

- Windflower (anemone canadensis) (uh-NEM-oh-nee ka-na-DEN-sis)

- Woodruff, Sweet (galium odoratum) (GAL-ee-um oh-dor-AH-tum)

The following are poisonous to ingest, so don't plant these around pets or young children. Note that this list includes both Spring and Fall plants.

- Bloodroot (sanguinaria canadensis) (san-gwin-AR-ee-uh ka-na-DEN-sis)

- Bush, Lily of the Valley (pieris japonica) (pee-AIR-iss juh-PON-ih-kuh) leaves and flowers

- Coralberry "Snowberry" (symphoricarpos albus) (sim-for-ee-KAR-poss AL-bus)

- Creeper, Trumpet (campsis radicans)KAMP-sis RAD-ee-kans) honorable mention for itchiness from skin contact

- Devil's Walking Stick (aralia spinosa) (uh-RAY-lee-uh spy-NO-suh) bark can irritate skin

- Four O'Clock (mirabilis jalapa) (mih-RAB-ih-liss juh-LAP-a)

- Foxglove (digitalis purpurea) (dij-ee-TAH-liss pur-PUR-ee-uh) leaves

- Gas Plant (dictamnus alba) (dik-TAM-nus AL-ba) honorable mention for allergic reactions from contact with oil

- Jack-in-the-Pulpit (arisaema triphyllum) (air-uh-SEE-muh try-FIL-um) roots

- Larkspur (consolida ambigua) (kon-SO-lih-duh am-BIG-yoo-uh) leaves, flowers, and roots if ingested

- Monkshood (aconitum) (a-kon-EYE-tum) ingestion or even touch is dangerous

- Rhubarb (rheum) (REE-um) leaves

- Rose, Christmas or Lenten (helleborus nigra) (hell-eh-BORE-us NY-gruh)

- Rue (ruta graveolens) (ROO-tuh grav-ee-OH-lens) leaves

- Sassafras (sassafras albidium) (SASS-uh-frass AL-bi-dum) carcinogenic oil

- Solomon's Seal, Fragrant (polygonatum) (po-lig-oh-NAY-tum)

- Spurge (euphorbia amygdaloides) (yoo-FOR-bee-uh am-ig-duh-LOY-deez) honorable mention for sap's skin irritation

- Squill, Siberian (scilla siberica) (SKI-uh sy-BEER-ah-kuh)

- Yew, Japanese Plum (cephalotaxus harringtonia) (se-uh-loh-TAKS-us har-ring-TOH-nee-uh) The berries are edible but the rest is toxic.

Chapter Seven

Bonus Section: Rabbit-Resistant Plants

These plants are deer-resistant, of course, but also rabbit-resistant. Detailed notes are above, so you will find only their common and Latin names listed here.

- Boxwood (buxus sempervirens)

- Bush, Butterfly (buddleia davidii)

- Candytuft (iberis sempervirens)

- Cotoneaster (cotoneaster)

- Cotoneaster Bearberry (cotoneaster dammeri)

- Crown Imperial (fritillaria imperialis 'lutea')

- Daffodil (narcissus)

- Dogwood, Flowering (cornus)

- Hyacinth (hyacinthus)

- Laurel, Mountain (kalmia)

- Lilac, Common (syringa vulgaris)

- Lily, Turf (lirope spicata)

- Maple, Full Moon (acer japonicum o-isami)

- Rhododendron (rhododendron)

- Sumac, Fragrant (rhus aromatica)

- Sweet-Gum (liquidambar styraciflua)

- Tree, Tulip (liriodendron tulipifera)

Definitions

Annual: living only one growing season, as beans or corn.

Biennial: completing its normal term of life in two years, flowering and fruiting the second year, as beets or winter wheat.

Bulb: 1) a usually subterranean and often globular bud having fleshy leaves emergent at the top and a stem reduced to a flat disk, rooting from the underside, as in the onion and lily; 2) a plant growing from such a bud.

Ground Cover: 1) the herbaceous plants and low shrubs in a forest, considered as a whole; 2) any of a variety of low-growing or trailing plants used to cover the ground in areas where grass is difficult to grow, as in dense shade or on steep slopes.

Hardy: able to withstand the cold of winter in the open air.

Herb: a flowering plant whose stem above ground does not become woody, especially if such a plant when valued for its medicinal properties, flavor, scent, or the like.

Perennial: a plant having a life cycle of more than two years.

Shrub: a woody plant smaller than a tree, usually having multiple permanent stems branching from or near the ground.

Tree: a woody perennial plant, typically having a single stem or trunk growing to a considerable height and bearing lateral branches at some distance from the ground:

Vine: 1) any plant having a long, slender stem that trails or creeps on the ground or climbs by winding itself about a support or holding fast with tendrils or claspers; 2) the stem of any such plant.

References

Better Homes and Gardens http://www.bhg.com/gardening/plant-dictionary

Curtis, Paul D., Cornell Cooperative Extension Monroe County and Richmond, Milo E., New York Cooperative Fish and Wildlife Research Unit. Reducing Deer Damage to Ornamental and Garden Plants. (2018)

"Deer-resistant Trees and Shrubs for Iowa,"

http://www.dictionary.com

Fast Growing Trees https://www.fast-growing-trees.com/collections/deer-resistant

Finnegran, Rebecca. Winter deer damage heavy? Seek deer-resistant plants. (2015) Michigan State University http://www.msu.edu

Gurneys http://www.gurneys.com

Indiana deer-resistant plants and repellants Indiana University

http://www.deerfriendly.com/deer.indiana-deer-resistant-plants-and-repellents

Missouri Botanical Garden

Nuisance Wildlife Repellent Handbook. Minnesota Department of Natural Resources, Wildlife Damage Management Program

Plants not Favored by Deer. The Morton Arboretum, https://mortonarb.org/plant-and-protect/tree-plant-care/plant-care-resources/plants-not-favored-by-deer/

Nuisance Wildlife Repellent Handbook. Minnesota Department of Natural Resources, Wildlife Damage Management Program

Rutgers http://www.njaes.rutgers.edu/deer-resistant plants

Spring Hill Nursery www.springhillnursery.com

The Top Deer- Resistant Plants for the Midwest. (2016) https://bhg.com/gardening/gardening-by-region/midwest/the-top-deer-resistant-plants-for-the-midwest

University of Illinois, Extension https://web.extension.illinois.edu/perennials/specific

http://www.extension.illinois.edu/blogs/good-growing/2018-05-17-oh-deer

University of Minnesota, Extension http://www.extension.umn.edu/yard-and-garden

https://extension.umn.edu/planting-and-growing-guides/white-tailed-deer-damage

USDA Plant Hardiness Zone Map https://planthardiness.ars.usda.gov/pages/view-maps

Lady Bird Johnson Wildflower Center- The University of Texas at Austin

Flowering Shrubs for the Hudson Valley

North Carolina State Extension Gardener Plant Toolbox

Pros and Cons of Popular Types of Deer Fencing by David Beaulieu,

The Complete Encyclopedia of Natural Healing, Gary Null, Bottom Line Books, 2008.

55 Most Common Medicinal Herbs, Second Edition, Heather Boon and Michael Smith, Robert Rose, 2009.

Links to Useful Sites

Look at the interactive USDA Zone map here:

https://planthardiness.ars.usda.gov/pages/view-maps

These links to sunrise times, sunset times, and day length may come in handy when you're deciding when to bring those plants inside for the winter.

https://sunrise-sunset.org/calendar

https://www.suntoday.org/sunrise-sunset/2021.html

This site tells you how to pronounce Latin names:

http://www.davesgarden.com/botanary

Acknowledgments

I WOULD LIKE TO thank my friend (of almost sixty years!) Mary Golden for her emotional support and proofreading. I would also like to thank my sister Lorna Allard and my friend Terri Pattio for their encouragement.

Also by Sue Monson

Deer-Resistant Gardening in the Midwest: Spring Planting Edition, Almennigen Enterprises, 2022.